MW00587902

SATELLITES

BY DIANA SON

★

★

DRAMATISTS
PLAY SERVICE
INC.

SATELLITES
Copyright © 2008, Diana Son

All Rights Reserved

NOTE ON BILLING

SPECIAL NOTE ON SONGS/RECORDINGS

2

for Wilder, Nate and Dash

SATELLITES was produced by The Public Theater (Mara Manus, Executive Director; Oskar Eustis, Artistic Director) in New York City, opening on June 6, 2006. It was directed by Michael Greif; the set design was by Mark Wendland; the costume design was by Miranda Hoffman; the lighting design was by Kenneth Posner; the sound design was by Walter Trarbach and Tony Smolenski IV; the production stage manager was Martha Donaldson; and the assistant stage manager was Sharika Niles. The cast was as follows:

NINA .... Sandra Oh
MILES .... Kevin Carroll
ERIC .... Clarke Thorell
KIT .... Johanna Day
MRS. CHAE .... Satya Lee
REGGIE .... Ron Cephas Jones
WALTER .... Ron Brice

5

CHARACTERS

NINA, mid-30s, Korean-American, an architect and new mother

MILES, mid-30s, African-American, an unemployed dot-com casualty and new father

ERIC, late 30s, Caucasian, Miles' brother, an entrepreneur

KIT, late 30s, Caucasian, Nina's business partner, an architect

MRS. CHAE, early 50s/early 60s, Korean from Korea, a nanny

REGGIE, early/mid-40s, African-American, the king of the block

PLACE

Various rooms in Miles' and Nina's
unrenovated Brooklyn brownstone.

TIME

2000s.

NOTE: (.) denotes a barely perceptible (and yet perceptible) pause where a character chooses not to say something.

SATELLITES

Scene 1

Late night/early morning — they've bled into one another. Nina, still tender from a C-section, bounces her two-week-old newborn as best as she can and pats her back, trying to soothe the crying baby.

NINA. OK, sweetie it's OK. I'm trying, I'm trying — *(Reacting to harder crying.)* I'm sorry it hurts so much — *(Nina pats harder.)* You know, if only it were this hard for adults to fart, riding the subway would be a much pleasanter — *(We hear the tiny pop of a baby passing a puff of gas. Nina reacts with the pride of a mother who's just watched her daughter win Olympic gold. The baby makes a happy, gurgling sound.)* You did it! Oh, I'm so happy for you! *(Nina holds the baby in front of her to look at her face. She gives her an encouraging little shake.)* My little champion! *(The baby starts to cry again. To herself, out loud:)* Holy shit, don't shake the baby. I'm such a fucking — *(She puts the baby back over her shoulder.)* Mommy didn't mean that, Mommy wasn't shaking you, Mommy was … vibrating you — *(Miles walks in, wearing pajamas.)*
MILES. I can't believe I didn't hear you guys, I was out cold. Did she want to nurse?
NINA. *(Not ironic.)* No, she wanted to watch *The Godfather*. Did you know that the *The Godfather* is on every night? On different channels at the same time. If you turn on your TV after midnight, you have no choice but to watch *The Godfather*.
MILES. You want to watch it now?
NINA. Why don't you take the baby, so I can go back to bed. *(Nina carefully puts the baby in Miles' arms. The baby starts to cry harder.)* Look at her, Miles, chocolate skin, almond eyes … she's the best of both of us.

MILES. ... I hope so.

NINA. What do you think about hiring a Korean woman to be her nanny? So she could speak Korean to her.

MILES. *(Distracted by crying baby.)* Uh, OK. I didn't know you —

NINA. I just started thinking about it. I can't speak Korean so she's not going to hear it from me.

MILES. Alright, sounds like a good idea. *(Re: baby.)* You want to take her? I think she wants —

NINA. Why don't you try singing a song? Like a lullaby or something.

MILES. *(Sings.)* "The eensy-weensy spider went up the water — "

NINA. That's not soothing. *(A bang from the apartment above.)*

MILES. Aw, come on, man.

NINA. Fucking asshole. *(To upstairs neighbor.)* My baby has gas, man, I'll kill you, motherfucker.

MILES. Hopefully we'll close on the house next month, and finally be able to move in.

NINA. It's impossible to have a baby in this cramped little tenement. We've outgrown this apartment, this whole neighborhood.

MILES. Remember when we used to make fun of our friends who moved to Brooklyn?

NINA. They're laughing at us now. Still, as much as we paid, it'll be worth it. *(The baby wails, the neighbor bangs on the ceiling again.)*

MILES. You'd better take her. *(Nina opens her arms. The baby quiets down a little.)*

NINA. What should I sing? *(Miles thinks a beat.)*

MILES. *(Sings.)* "Hush little baby — " *(Nina joins in, a beat behind, following Miles.)*

MILES and NINA. "Don't say a word, Papa's gonna buy you a mockingbird ... "

MILES. "If that — "

NINA. "When that — "

MILES and NINA. " ... mockingbird won't sing, Papa's gonna buy you a — " *(They look at each other, unsure what the rest of the words are. Finally —)*

NINA. I can look up the words, I found this website that has the lyrics to all the —

MILES. *(Sings, cues Nina.)* "Rock-a-bye — " *(Nina joins in.)*

MILES and NINA. *(Singing.)* " — baby, on the treetop. When the wind blows, the cradle will rock. When the bough breaks, the cradle will fall — " *(Nina stops, thinks about the words.)*

MILES. *(Still singing.)* "And down will come baby, cradle and all."

NINA. We are never singing that song to her again.

MILES. Why not?

NINA. The baby falls, Miles, the baby falls and the cradle falls on top of it. What kind of lullaby is that?

Scene 2

Miles' and Nina's unrenovated brownstone. It's dark, lit by a standing lamp. The living room blends into the kitchen, a stairwell leads to the bedrooms above, another connects to the garden level office below. Many moving boxes are piled on the floor, some opened, most not. There is very little furniture. Miles carries in a box as Nina comes down the stairs.

NINA. I just got her down. Miles, that box belongs in the kitchen. It says "Kitchen" on it.

MILES. It doesn't matter. I've been putting things wherever there's room.

NINA. Well, I've been putting everything exactly where it's/gonna go —

MILES. But I haven't. We'll deal with it later. *(Nina grabs an end of the box, starts pulling towards the kitchen. Miles pulls it back.)*

NINA. You know we won't. Half of these boxes are going to be sitting in our living room for the next year and a half because we're not going to have the time or energy to/move them later.

MILES. We'll move them tomorrow. Or next week … or next month, it doesn't —

NINA. No, we're not. We'll get used to them being there. We'll start putting things on them, like our feet when we're sitting on the sofa. Or our drinks, they'll become end tables. We'll choose the paint color for the walls by whether or not it matches the boxes. You know we will.

MILES. No, we won't.

NINA. How many years did we use a plastic shopping bag hanging on the front doorknob as a garbage can? Seven years. I bought us our first trash can on my thirtieth birthday because I couldn't stand it anymore. Miles, please, let's just move the goddamn box to the kitchen. I need to finish here and go downstairs to —

MILES. Stop bossing me around. *(Nina starts to pull the box towards the kitchen again, Miles resists. She stops in her tracks when she feels a cutting pain. She drops her half of the box.)*

NINA. Ow, motherfuck. *(Miles sets the box down, walks over to her, helps her to sit onto a nearby box.)*

MILES. Honey ... you shouldn't be doing all this. You need to stop pushing yourself so much.

NINA. I'm not pushing *myself,* Miles.

MILES. So, what — I am?

NINA. There's no one else to help us. We've burned through all the friends who offered to ... let's just finish. After I'm done here, I have to go downstairs and help Kit work on the site plan.

MILES. You're gonna work tonight?

NINA. Kit's been carrying my weight for the past month. *(Miles starts to massage Nina's shoulders.)* She's been working on the Tillman job and on the Barcelona competition. Not to mention she set up the whole office by herself.

MILES. Yeah, well, Kit can do that. She has the time. You should just ... take it easy, you know? Relax a little. *(Miles touches Nina's breasts. She wriggles out of his reach.)* Hey!

NINA. I'm sorry ... honey, it's just ... these aren't mine anymore.

MILES. Nina, I've been keeping it all to myself here for the past four months.

NINA. What're you — counting? *(Miles tries to nuzzle her.)*

MILES. C'mon, the baby's asleep.

NINA. I can't believe I just told you everything I have to do tonight and you want to have sex?

MILES. Yes, I want to have sex! Remember sex? It's how we made the baby and got ourselves into this mess in the first place.

NINA. That's seductive. *(Miles lets go of her hand, walks away angry and rejected.)*

MILES. I'll get the rest of the boxes myself. You just ... relax.

NINA. I don't have time to —

MILES. You need to —

NINA. I'm not relaxing! — *(Eric runs into the house, shuts the door behind him. His jacket pocket is torn. Miles and Nina look as surprised to see him as he is to see them —)*

ERIC. Two fucking guys just chased me for four blocks. They took my ipod and backpack, they had a gun!

NINA. Eric! Where did you —

MILES. Are you OK? You want me to call the cops?

ERIC. Yeah, no, it's OK, I just — *(He walks over to the window, looks out.)*

MILES. Where was this?

ERIC. Like a block from the subway, by the projects. All of a sudden, these two (.) guys came up from behind me and ripped my ipod out of my pocket — *(Nina examines Eric's pocket.)*

MILES. Did they get your wallet?

ERIC. No, I have a hole in my pocket so it drops down into the lining of my coat. They grabbed my backpack, and then I just … took off. I just kept running until I saw Rosa Parks Avenue.

NINA. How'd you know how to get here?

MILES. You want a glass of water or something? A beer?

ERIC. In a minute, I just — *(Changing gears.)* Hi, how are you? *(Eric kisses Nina on the cheek.)*

NINA. I'm fine. *(Miles and Eric embrace, clap each other on the back.)*

MILES. I thought you were in Malaysia.

ERIC. I just got off the plane. I'm fucking lagged.

NINA. Where are your bags?

ERIC. I put them in a mini-storage near the airport. *(Looks around.)* Get a load of this place. What's the deal?

MILES. … This is … our house.

ERIC. This is outrageous, man, your other apartment was like a dorm room. How many floors is this?

NINA. Four. We converted the garden level into an office for me and Kit so, we're only living on this floor and the one above.

ERIC. That where the bedrooms are?

NINA. Yes.

ERIC. So how many bedrooms are there?

NINA. Three. We use the third one as a family office.

MILES. *My* office.

ERIC. Sweet, man. Mom and Dad said it was nice but I didn't expect it would be like this.

MILES. Why, what'd they say?

ERIC. Don't sweat it, Miles, they liked it. They were just more into the baby. Where'd you put the baby?

NINA. She's upstairs sleeping.

ERIC. Can I get a peek at her?

MILES. Sure.

NINA. I don't think it's a good idea.

ERIC. How old is she, a month?

MILES. Six weeks.

ERIC. Is she sleeping through the night?

NINA. *(On the verge of tears.)* No!

MILES. *(An apology.)* The baby gets up every couple hours to nurse. Nina's up all night.

ERIC. I noticed the moving van out front. You guys need a hand?

MILES. You don't have to, man, you must be exhausted.

ERIC. Getting mugged got me pumped. Let's do it, man. *(Kit walks upstairs carrying a pizza box.)*

KIT. Your pizza came, they rang the bell downstairs.

MILES. *(Turns to Eric.)* Let's eat something first. *(To Kit.)* Kit, you've met my brother before, haven't you? Eric? *(Kit extends her hand.)*

KIT. Not yet, but I've heard the stories.

ERIC. Uh-oh ...

KIT. You've been bitten by a rattlesnake and lived to tell the tale, and you sold the Dalai Lama a laptop.

ERIC. His Holiness is addicted to Tetris.

KIT. *(To Nina.)* Nina, I've started regrading the site plan.

NINA. I told you I'd pitch in with that.

KIT. We've got to finish this by tonight. We should be cutting out shapes for the model by tomorrow.

NINA. We will. I'm going to work all day tomorrow.

ERIC. *(To Kit.)* Are you guys doing a charette?

MILES. Listen to you and your "charette."

ERIC. *(To Miles.)* Just because I didn't go to *Columbia*, like some of us in the room —

MILES. All of us, actually. *(Nina's mobile phone rings. Miles and Eric help themselves to pizza.)*

NINA. *(Checking phone, to Kit.)* Audrey Tillman.

KIT. Why's she calling *you*?

NINA. *(Into phone.)* Hello? Yes, Mrs. Tillman ... no, I wasn't at the jobsite today but Kit was — *(Nina looks at Kit, who nods, yes, I was, everything was fine.)* No, the carpenters are going to fill that in ... It's going to look exactly as we discussed. *(Brightens.)* Oh, yes, thank you. She's six weeks old, she's just starting to — *(Mrs. Tillman could give a fuck.)* I'll make sure Kit takes a look tomorrow morning. Thank you, Mrs. Till — *(Mrs. Tillman has hung up.)*

KIT. Why didn't she call me? I'm the one whose been holding her shriveled little liver-spotted hand for the past two [months] — *(The baby starts crying upstairs. Nina reacts as if she's been electrically jolted.)*

NINA. You guys, go ahead, eat. I'll bring her down when I'm done nursing her.

KIT. I guess I'll be working by myself after all. *(Eric hands Kit a slice of pizza on a plate.)*

ERIC. Here you go. *(He goes to the fridge to get her a beer. Miles touches Kit consolingly.)* So, do you live in Brooklyn too? *(Eric hands her a beer.)*

KIT. Ha! Thanks. Noooo. Look, Brooklyn's great, it's beautiful *and* cheaper, but … I want to be able to drop off my dry cleaning, go to a gallery opening, see an eight-hour Hungarian movie, then drink overpriced green apple martinis — all within a block of my house.

ERIC. That's what's great about New York, right? *(Suddenly, we hear a smash — the sound of glass being shattered and falling on the floor.)*

MILES. What the — *(Kit grabs a flashlight, they see glass pieces on the floor and a jagged hole in the window.)*

ERIC. Shit, man —

MILES. What just happened? *(Kit walks towards the window, surveys the debris. Finds a rock, picks it up.)*

KIT. It's a rock. Someone just threw it at your window. *(Miles walks over, Kit shows him the rock.)*

MILES. Why would someone do that?

ERIC. You've got a stereo, TV, all kinds of computer equipment … people in this neighborhood probably saw all that gear and thought Puffy was moving in.

KIT. Or, maybe they weren't trying to steal anything. Maybe they were just trying to send you a message. *(Goes for phone.)* Want me to call 911? *(Nina walks a few steps downstairs.)*

NINA. Miles? What was that, what broke?

MILES. Stay upstairs, honey. There's broken glass down here. *(Nina, holding the baby, walks down, sees the broken glass on the floor.)*

NINA. Fucking motherfucker. Who broke my fucking window?

MILES. I'm checking it out, don't worry. Go back upstairs where it's safe. *(Nina takes a few steps into the living room.)*

NINA. It's going to take weeks to get a fucking replacement glass … what are we supposed to do with a fucking hole in our house for three fucking weeks?

MILES. *I don't know.* Just take the baby upstairs, OK? *(To Eric.)* Her first word's gonna be fuck if Nina keeps —

NINA. What?

MILES. Just please take the baby upstairs. *(She goes upstairs.)*

KIT. You should call the cops, Miles. *(Beat.)*

MILES. I don't want to do that. We're new here. I don't want peo-

13

ple to get the wrong impression.

KIT. What would that be?

MILES. I don't want to dwell on this. The most important thing to do is cover up that hole.

KIT. Home Depot's open twenty-four hours. You can buy a four-by-eight piece of plywood and some hardware to anchor it to the wall.

ERIC. I'll go. Will you come with me so you can show me?

KIT. I'll get my jacket. *(Miles shakes his brother's hand.)*

MILES. Thanks, man. Can you believe this happened? *(Eric looks out the window, at the sky.)*

ERIC. It's a full moon. Maybe it's a sign of good luck.

MILES. Or it's a sign that moving my family here is the biggest mistake of my life. *(Kit comes back with her jacket, she and Eric walk out, leaving Miles alone and feeling it.)*

Scene 3

Early morning. Miles tries to set the plywood into the wall, manual labor is not his forte. Eric sleeps on a nearby couch. A man walks by on the street, Reggie, his clothes not quite clean, his hair in need of a comb. He stops in front of the broken window. The hole still uncovered.

REGGIE. Oh, shit! What happened, man?

MILES. What happened? Somebody smashed the window.

REGGIE. And you ain't hardly even moved in yet — that ain't a way to welcome a brother to the neighborhood. *(Miles — a small reaction to "brother.")*

MILES. It's not exactly a pie on the stoop, is it?

REGGIE. That's what I'm saying! You done a lot of work on this house, man.

MILES. Well, we bought a door and … we put glass in the —

REGGIE. We got all kinds of people up in here now, building new condos and renovatin' these old brownstones … You see that house over there? Two homosexuals bought that, fixed it up to historical accuracy, and all that. I'm glad you came to the neighborhood, man. What you do, you a lawyer or something?

14

MILES. I'm … an interactive producer.

REGGIE. A producer! You know Biggie grew up two blocks from here, right? I used to send that punk to the store to buy me Milk Duds.

MILES. Actually, I produce websites and DVD-ROMs for corporate clients. But, I like Biggie.

REGGIE. I'm glad you came to the neighborhood, man. This glass was custom-made, wasn't it?

MILES. *(A little surprised.)* Yeah, it was.

REGGIE. 'Cause 'round here all the brownstones have one seventy-two-inch window or two thirty-six-inch ones. That was the style in the 1870s when most of these buildings was built. But this one here is eighty inches, only one like it. I know they charged you a lot of money for that piece of glass. *(Miles waits to see where Reggie's going with this.)* Mm-hm, a lot of money. *(Reggie nods gravely.)*

MILES. You seem to know a lot about my house —

REGGIE. I got a guy I can go to — he'll cut that glass for you cheaper than you paid for.

MILES. Thanks, but my wife's got her sources. She's an architect so she has reliable [vendors] —

REGGIE. *(Insistent.)* Listen, man, you don't know me. But, I'm telling you — *(Extends his hand.)* I'm Reggie, I live across the street from you, I lived on this block for — matter of fact, I was born on this block. I'm forty-two years old — I got three grown kids, they live with they moms, but everybody 'round here know Reggie. If you need something, I'm your boy. *(Nina walks downstairs carrying the baby.)*

NINA. Miles, you take the baby. Kit's going to be here any — *(To Reggie.)* Hi, I'm Nina. *(She can't offer her hand because she's holding the baby.)*

REGGIE. Alright.

MILES. This is Reggie, he lives across the street.

REGGIE. *(To Miles.)* Like I said, you make up your mind, you come to me. *(Miles, feeling awkward, turns to Nina.)*

MILES. Oh, I should tell you, Reggie mentioned that he, uh, he has a glazier that he recommends.

NINA. He's done work for you?

REGGIE. *(A nod.)* Mm-hm.

NINA. Do you have his card or can you give me his phone number?

MILES. *(To Nina.)* I thought you would want to use Frankie again.

NINA. I'll call Frankie, but if this guy's in the neighborhood —

(Reggie sees someone offstage.)

REGGIE. I gotta talk to this — Hey, Mo! You need to settle up with me, son. *(To Miles.)* Look, I'm a go get my boy's card and you talk to him. Whatever you want, he'll do it.

NINA. Thanks, Reggie. *(To Miles.)* I don't know what kind of work this guy does, I'm just saying let's get a price from him.

MILES. Doesn't it seem weird to you, this guy who's always hanging out on the corner, coming up first thing in the morning, telling us, "I got a guy who can fix that for you … "

NINA. So?

MILES. And where were those guys last night? They're always out there, doing whatever they're doing, *selling* whatever they're selling, but last night — they're not there. Where were they?

NINA. What — you think Reggie or one of those guys broke the glass? *(Miles gestures — I'm just saying.)* … I don't think Reggie did it. Why would he do it?

MILES. Maybe he gets a fee. Whenever Reggie finds some sucker to give this guy business —

NINA. And what's the deal with your brother? He tell you how long he's gonna stay?

MILES. No. But he usually stays a week or two — you have a problem with that? *(Nina turns to the baby for unconditional love.)*

NINA. *(Turns to baby.)* Look, she's dreaming. Look at how her expression changes every couple seconds. *(Narrating the baby's thoughts as she goes from a smile, to a frown, to tears, to a smile again.)* Flowers … car alarms … mmm, Mommy's nipples … *(Eric comes downstairs.)*

ERIC. Alright, let me see her. *(Looks at baby.)* She's beautiful.

NINA. She's the perfect mix of the both of us, don't you think?

ERIC. She's herself. You, on the other hand, seem to have turned into a completely different person. Didn't I just hear you talking baby talk?

NINA. I was giving voice to her thoughts.

ERIC. Can I hold her? *(Nina hesitates.)*

MILES. Of course, man.

NINA. Just — make sure you support her neck. *(Nina gingerly hands the baby to Eric.)*

ERIC. Ohmigod, it's so much responsibility. If I don't hold her right, her neck will break off. *(Miles goes to get a camera.)*

MILES. Hang on a second, let me take a picture of you two.

NINA. Miles — don't put him on the spot.

ERIC. I don't mind. *(Eric smiles for the camera. Miles clicks the shutter. Nina responds to the sound of the downstairs door being opened.)*

NINA. Shit, Kit's here. I'd wanted to get a head start before she showed up. Miles, take the baby.

MILES. Eric's got her.

NINA. *(To Miles.)* You said you'd watch the baby today —

MILES. I will. But, just today. Remember I have an interview at Poseidon tomorrow — *(Nina heads downstairs.)*

ERIC. You guys don't have a nanny?

MILES. Not yet. But we'd better soon, because I can't go on interviews if I'm stuck here taking care of the baby.

ERIC. Look at you man, you've got a wife, a kid, *a house* ... Not just any house, a Brooklyn brownstone.

MILES. Yeah, but it needs a lot of work, man. I mean, this kitchen is like, from *Sanford and Son*. This linoleum floor ... I was gonna fix it but then we ran out of money.

ERIC. What do you mean you ran out of money — look at this place, you're swimming in bucks.

MILES. Look at this place, exactly. I don't even want to tell you how much we paid for it. I had to cash in the last of my stock options for the down payment. If it weren't for the income we get renting the top floor apartment, we couldn't afford to live here.

ERIC. There's another apartment?

MILES. On the fourth floor. Eventually, we hope to take it over but right now we need the money.

ERIC. You've got something set aside, I know you, Miles. You've probably got ten thousand dollars in quarters all rolled up and stuffed inside a pair of tube socks upstairs.

MILES. Dude, InTech laid me off six weeks before the baby was born. Nina's the only one making a steady check now — *(Eric holds the baby with one hand, undoes his pants with the other.)*

ERIC. Check this out. This is what I got for spending three months in a tropical Asian paradise. *(Eric's pants crumple around his ankles, revealing small piles of blue currency rubber-banded around each leg.)*

MILES. What the hell are those?

ERIC. Ringgits. I sold hot dog carts to street vendors in Kuala Lumpur. This is my take home. Twenty-two thousand ringgits. Which is about five thousand U.S. dollars.

MILES. What're you, waiting to deposit them in Chicago?

ERIC. Oh. Did I say I was going back to Chicago? My building went co-op so they kicked me out. How are the rents in this neighborhood? Think I could find a one-bedroom in the six-hundred-to seven-hundred-dollar range?

MILES. Aw, no, man, maybe three years ago but now —

ERIC. Fucking yuppies coming in, jacking up the rents so that even a guy like me can't afford to live in the ghetto. *(A smile, he pats Miles on the back.)*

MILES. It isn't exactly the [ghetto] —

ERIC. I'm just kidding, man.

MILES. I know it's still rough around the edges, but, it's got a good history. A lot of families have been in these brownstones for six or seven generations. You've got teachers, artists, musicians — Biggie grew up a couple blocks from here.

ERIC. I get it, man.

MILES. It'll be good for Hannah to grow up around (.) ... all kinds of kids.

ERIC. It's a great place to start a business. What does this neighborhood need?

MILES. We have to drive two neighborhoods over to get organic milk.

ERIC. What else?

MILES. You know — pasta sauce, good cheese, bread ...

ERIC. So, a place where you can buy upscale groceries, sit down and get a good cup of coffee, and — meet other people like you in the neighborhood.

MILES. Sounds good, man, I hope someone opens one.

ERIC. Why not you?

MILES. The thing I need to do right now is get a job. Bring some money into this house. Starting a business *costs* money.

ERIC. That's what investors are for.

MILES. Plus, it's risky.

ERIC. Man, don't you know you're taking a bigger risk waiting around for the right position to open up in the right company. Starting a business you gives you control. Look, I've got these ringgits. We can use them to get us off the ground.

MILES. OK, I'll ... think about it, man. *(Walter, the tenant, walks in. He tries not to notice Miles and Eric, standing there in his underwear with the ringgits. He heads up the stairs.)*

ERIC. Who the hell is that?

MILES. That's the tenant, Walter.

ERIC. He walks through your house to get to his apartment? That is weird, man. Come on, let's take a walk around the neighborhood. Scope out some old storefronts. I'll carry the baby.

MILES. We can't leave with the window like that.

ERIC. It'll be fine. We'll be back in ten minutes. We can work on it then. *(Miles picks up the Baby Björn.)*

MILES. You want to wear the Björn?

ERIC. No, man. I don't want that thing. Think about it — two dudes walking down the street with a mixed-race baby in a Baby Björn? It's not like people are gonna guess we're brothers. I'll just carry her like this, OK? *(Eric holds Hannah in the football hold.)*

MILES. She hasn't made a peep this whole time, she likes you.

ERIC. Of course she likes me, man. I'm crazy Uncle Eric. She needs me.

MILES. For what?

ERIC. To be everything you're not. *(They exit.)*

Scene 4

Nina, holding Hannah, sits across from Mrs. Chae, who is dressed neatly and paying a little more attention to Hannah than Nina.

NINA. I didn't expect to have to go back to work so soon. The good thing is I get to work at home — unlike other working mothers who have to go to their midtown [offices] —

MRS. CHAE. *(Korean accent.)* Yes, I know. My daughter is lawyer and she [works] —

NINA. But, most working mothers get three months maternity leave and I have to start working after only six weeks. My partner and I have made it to the finals in a major design [competition] —

MRS. CHAE. These days, woman *has* to work. My daughter says —

NINA. — A major design competition for a new arts center in Barcelona. *(She looks to Mrs. Chae for approval, signs she's impressed. She gets none. Clearing throat:)* Arts Center in Barcelona. It's an international competition and only four groups made it to the final. It's an honor and a huge — *(Mrs. Chae makes clicking noises at the baby.)* Anyway, the deadline is in six weeks so that's why I need a nanny to start right away —

19

MRS. CHAE. Can I hold her? *(Nina unconsciously hesitates.)*

NINA. Yes, of course, just — be careful of/her [neck] —

MRS. CHAE. *(Soothing to Nina.)* I know ... I know ... *(Mrs. Chae takes the baby, while saying in Korean, "Oh, look at you, you're such a pretty girl." This unexpectedly touches Nina.)* Your mommy and daddy must be very happy.

NINA. I think my dad liked her, it's hard to tell.

MRS. CHAE. But your mommy, she was so proud.

NINA. No, Mommy's dead.

MRS. CHAE. Tsk tsk tsk. You take care of baby, your mommy supposed take care of you. *(This moves Nina again. The baby makes a sound. Mrs. Chae immediately soothes her by patting her on the back and saying a few words in Korean.)*

NINA. She's smiling at you.

MRS. CHAE. Babies love me. And I love the babies too. The family I worked for before? Husband got the new job in Ohio. They ask me to move with them, "Please, nanny, come with us." But I cannot go. I have my family here. I have a grandson, did you know?

NINA. Oh, how old is he?

MRS. CHAE. My daughter, she work at big law firm, they have daycare center in building. I told my daughter, "I quit my job to take care of him, he's my grandson." But she say, "Mommy, don't be selfish, I want him near me."

NINA. Her name is Hannah, did I tell you?

MRS. CHAE. I think maybe you name her Hannah *(Pronounces it huh-NAH.)* because she's first one born.

NINA. Actually, we just liked the name. And it's HA-nah, not huh-NAH. That would be weird, wouldn't it? Naming her "number one"?

MRS. CHAE. You know Huh-nah?

NINA. *(Counts in Korean, pronunciation shaky.)* Hana, tul, set ...

MRS. CHAE. Oh. Because when you tell me you don't speak one word of Korean, I think you don't speak one word.

NINA. I do know *one word*. I know *"hana."* Actually, I can count to ten, my parents *did* teach me that. I just don't know how to say ... eleven or twelve. I don't know any Korean lullabies, or how to say "koochie koo — "

MRS. CHAE. *(Starts to sing; insert first couple lines from "Koyangi Pom.")* Your mommy sang this to you.

NINA. *(Moved, wishing she wasn't.)* Yes, I think she did.

MRS. CHAE. *(Looking at Hannah.)* She has the curly hair.

NINA. Yes, from my husband. I'm thrilled. *(Mrs. Chae looks at the baby again.)*

MRS. CHAE. She looks like … your husband?

NINA. I don't know. My family thinks she looks like my husband and my husband's family thinks she looks like me.

MRS. CHAE. Your husband … he is … architect too?

NINA. No, he's uh … he's a computer guy. *(Miles hurries in.)*

MILES. I'm sorry I'm late, the interview went long —

NINA. So, it must've gone well. Do you think you got the —

MILES. I'll … tell you later. *(To Mrs. Chae.)* Hi, I'm Miles. *(He goes to shake Mrs. Chae's hand, she bows.)*

NINA. Oh, uh, Miles, this is Mrs. Chae. Mrs. Chae, this is my husband Miles.

MRS. CHAE. *(Not skipping a beat.)* Congratulations. She is beautiful baby.

MILES. Thank you, thank you.

MRS. CHAE. So, you don't mind? Nina says she want the Korean nanny to speak Korean to Hannah. You don't worry?

MILES. No, I — I think it'd be great. I think it'd be wonderful for Hannah to understand Korean. You thought I might be worried?

MRS. CHAE. Maybe some American parent don't want the child to get confused or handicapped.

MILES. No, no, I think it's one-hundred-percent a good thing. *(Mrs. Chae looks at Hannah, then Nina and Miles.)*

MRS. CHAE. She is lucky baby. *(Miles smiles, puts his arm around Nina.)*

MILES. Hey, why don't I take a picture of you three together? *(Miles gets his camera.)*

NINA. Um … Miles? It's a little premature —

MILES. It'll be nice. *(Nina stands next to Mrs. Chae, not quite committed. Mrs. Chae holds Hannah closer and smiles into the camera.)* That's great. *(Flash. The doorbell rings. Nina turns to Mrs. Chae.)*

NINA. Thank you for your time. Let me walk you to the door.

MRS. CHAE. Should I call you tomorrow?

NINA. I'll call you, thank you.

MILES. *(Checking picture on camera.)* You guys look great together! *(Nina opens the door to let Mrs. Chae out, sees Reggie.)*

NINA. Oh, hi Reggie. Come on in. *(Mrs. Chae leaves as Reggie comes in carrying a large, ornate chandelier.)*

REGGIE. *(To Miles.)* Check this out, man. I just bought it for fifty bucks, I sell it to you for seventy-five.

MILES. Where did you get that?

REGGIE. I told you, I bought it. *(Looks at their ceiling.)* I see you got a hook where one used to be. All you got to do is slip it on. You got a ladder?

MILES. Listen, Reggie, thanks but, we don't want to buy that.

REGGIE. It ain't gone be that hard, here — *(He hands it to Miles, who reluctantly takes it. Reggie moves some boxes underneath the hook.)* I could probably reach it like this.

MILES. Can you get down, please? You're stepping on some fragile electronic equipment.

REGGIE. You got some computer stuff in here?

MILES. Can you just come down? *(Reggie steps down.)*

REGGIE. *(To Miles.)* So, I talked to my boy over at the glassworks, I told him it was a eighty-inch window and he says he can do it for fifteen hundred dollars.

NINA. *(To Reggie.)* Oh. Did you get his card? 'Cause I should talk to him about some details. *(Reggie digs through his pockets.)*

REGGIE. I got his card, I got his card, here — *(He hands her a folded piece of paper then turns back to Miles.)* But if you want to pull the trigger on this, tell *me*. I'll set it up for you. Even with my fee, you ain't paying what you'd pay if you walked in there yourself. *(Miles looks at Nina.)*

MILES. Your fee. That's part of the fifteen hundred.

REGGIE. *(Goes to fridge.)* Oh, shit. You still got that fridge? That ugly-ass fridge been here since the seventies. *(Reggie opens the fridge.)*

MILES. Do you mind?

REGGIE. You know, I been in your house before. Yeah, I been in here before. Had some *good* times up in here, man. The night of the blackout, 1977, city was coal-black. People were running around crazy, smashing store windows, grabbing up anything they could get — bananas, turntables, diapers … Me and my friends climbed through that window, lay down on our backs, and looked straight up, man, saw stars we never get to see — the constellations. Aquila the eagle; Cygnus the swan; Hercules the warrior — he took on the labors, man. He brought down the lion, the hydra, Cerberus, himself. After the riots is when the monsters took over this neighborhood — drug dealers, gangs, robbers. Hercules should've stuck around, we coulda used him. But when the power came back on, all the stars faded away. *(Miles hands Reggie the chandelier.)*

Scene 5

The office. There are two drafting tables and stools, a desk with a computer and printer. Kit and Nina are building the landscape their model will sit on. Kit finishes gluing on a layer of gator board and is waiting for Nina to cut out more shapes. Meanwhile, Nina is looking for something.

KIT. Nina, I'm ready for more shapes. What're you doing, what're you looking for?

NINA. A green and yellow receiving blanket. It was mine when I was a baby. I have this picture of my mom holding me in it ... *(Their office phone rings. Kit checks the caller ID.)*

KIT. Don't get it, it's Mrs. Tillman. She's called three times already.

NINA. Not about the wall again.

KIT. The first two calls were about the wall. The third call was about the bathroom. She said the light made the wall tiles look "too shiny." I am so sick of these overly-entitled, ignorant, tantrum-throwing rich people.

NINA. Me too. I just want to be one.

KIT. I want to be in a whole new league. Get the hell out of residential work, be rid of these idiots forever.

NINA. I wonder what Mrs. Chae is doing to try to soothe her. *(Kit listens, hears nothing.)*

KIT. Hannah's not crying.

NINA. She is, they're upstairs in the bedroom.

KIT. You're saying you can hear them two floors above? I can't hear anything.

NINA. *(Standing up.)* I'm gonna go up there and offer to nurse her —

KIT. *(Also standing.)* Nina, don't. Just ... leave her, it's disrespectful. If the baby really needed you ... or your breasts ... the nanny would bring her down here. I don't even think she's crying.

NINA. I hear her. Being a mother has given me superhero powers. And Hannah — Hannah can smell me from twenty feet away.

KIT. You measured?

NINA. I read it and I tested it. And her crying — it triggers my

23

milk. I was in the bathroom yesterday and she started crying, and milk shot out of my nipples. Smacked right into the back of the door. Sometimes my milk attacks her. *(We hear Hannah crying. Mrs. Chae has brought her downstairs to the living room. Nina looks at Kit.)*

KIT. No, Nina, concentrate. We blew the first two months of our deadline already. We have six weeks to do what all our competitors have had four months to do. I didn't mean blow.

NINA. I couldn't stand up —

KIT. I know, honey.

NINA. Any woman who has a planned C-section is a fucking moron.

KIT. I like the image of the doctor grabbing your intestines by the handful and piling them on your stomach, then shoving them back in after she gets the baby out. You know, I think you've broken some kind of sacred code of silence by telling me the details of your horrible birth experience.

NINA. Are you afraid to have a baby now?

KIT. Hell yeah! Not that it's an option right — *(Eric comes downstairs, puts a set of keys on Kit's desk.)*

ERIC. Thanks for letting me borrow these, Miles made a spare set for me.

KIT. No problem.

ERIC. Hey, you know that radio station you told me about? I tuned into it this morning. They play some great music.

KIT. I figured since you lost your ipod …

ERIC. I appreciate it. Well, I'll leave you gals to your work. *(Eric heads upstairs.)*

NINA. What the hell was that about? You loaned him your keys?

KIT. Yeah. What's wrong with that?

NINA. I don't want him getting too comfortable. I don't want him to be here at all. Eric is not the kind of person Miles should get into business with.

KIT. Why not?

NINA. He's never done anything legit, he's never had a proper job … and he's never been able to commit to a relationship.

KIT. That was unsolicited.

NINA. Stream of consciousness. The thing is, I think Miles is using Eric and this business as a way of avoiding having to spend time with the baby.

KIT. If you think that there's some guy out there who's going to do more than what Miles is doing … you're nuts.

NINA. Fucking Joe.

KIT. You think Joe's a shit because he wouldn't marry me after six years, but I think Joe's normal. Every guy in the world is like Joe. You've had it lucky Nina, you don't know —

NINA. How hard it is out there? It's hard in here. This is hard. *(Beat.)*

KIT. Last night, I went to a Salvadoran restaurant with this guy. I kept telling him in a nice way "It's not *El Salvadorean* food. It's Salvadoran." But all night he kept saying "I've never had El Salvadorean food before," "I have to tell my friends I went to an El Salvadorean restaurant."

NINA. Sounds like another online loser. Where was the restaurant?

KIT. Deepest Queens. To get there we had to take the Z train. The Z train to Jamaica Center. Then we had to walk twelve blocks to get to this little piece of shit restaurant that served the most heavenly pupusas made on the planet.

NINA. You bring some back for me?

KIT. No. Hot off the griddle — the crust was crisp and toothsome and when you bit into them the cheese and pork oozed —

NINA. Stop — *(Kit reaches into her desk, pulls out a bag of pupusas, tosses them to Nina.)*

KIT. They're not going to be as good cold, but — *(Miles comes downstairs.)*

MILES. Nina, have you seen my camcorder?

NINA. What? No.

MILES. I know I put it on the bookshelf yesterday but now I can't find it. I wanted to shoot some video of Hannah on her first day with Mrs. Chae.

NINA. You know what, Miles, there's a new rule. I want you to spread the word that this office is off-limits to anyone who doesn't work here.

MILES. What — ?

NINA. We're on a serious deadline here.

KIT. Yes, and it's ticking away every minute that you stand there arguing with your [husband] —

MILES. This office is part of *my house,* Nina —

NINA. Our house. But, Kit and I pay rent here.

MILES. You have to throw that in my face?

NINA. This is our space, Miles, and I don't want anyone else down here.

MILES. This is bullshit — *(He storms off.)*

NINA. *(Calling after him.)* Except Hannah and Mrs. Chae! They're still allowed to [come] — *(The office phone rings.)*

KIT. *(Into phone.)* Hello? What?! Javier, I told you twice before I left last night those pipes had to be flush with the I-beams — Alright, look, just tell Mrs. Tillman to put her ass on ice, I'll be there in an hour. *(Off his reaction.)* I'll take a cab, but I'm in fucking Brooklyn. *(She hangs up the phone, dials another number.)*

NINA. Want me to call a car service?

KIT. I'm already doing it. *(Into phone.)* Yeah, can I get a car at 127 Rosa Parks Avenue? Thanks.

NINA. I'll finish the shapes for the foundation by the time you — *(Mrs. Chae walks downstairs carrying the crying Hannah.)*

MRS. CHAE. I'm sorry, Nina, I try give her pacifier, I try my finger, I play nice music —

NINA. *(Looks to Kit.)* Can you take her for a walk outside? Could you try that?

MRS. CHAE. OK, yes, OK. I'm sorry I interrupt —

NINA. It's OK. *(Nina looks at Hannah, feeling she might lose her resolve, she turns away. Sound of a car horn outside. Mrs. Chae starts to leave, Hannah cries harder. Kit grabs her bag.)*

KIT. That's my car. If you finish the layers by the time I get back, we might be able to stay on schedule. *(One quick look at Nina, who continues working, then Kit's out the door. When Nina hears the door close, she stands up. She starts for the stairs — then stops, starts — stops ... then runs upstairs.)*

Scene 6

Afternoon. There are fewer moving boxes — the place looks more settled. The window is still broken, a piece of plywood has been anchored to the wall to cover it. Reggie walks in carrying two boxes of ceramic tiles and sets them down on the kitchen floor, near another open box, of a different shape. He can't resist looking into the other box. Miles walks in carrying another two boxes, sees Reggie.

MILES. Can I help you, man?

REGGIE. I see you got a X-Box. I can get you some games that

26

go with it real cheap. They still in the plastic, let me show you what I got — *(He starts for the door.)*

MILES. It's alright. I don't have time to play games these days.

REGGIE. They factory sealed. They ain't no cheap-ass Chinese — *(Oops. Reggie does a quick scan for Nina.)*

MILES. She's not Chinese. And if they're meant to be sold in a store, how'd you get them?

REGGIE. I got a guy, he works in a Circuit City. He say sometimes they order twenty-five copies of a game, they get twenty-six.

MILES. So, they're stolen.

REGGIE. How's it stolen, the store ain't paid for it!

MILES. If you take something from a store without paying for it. you stole it!

REGGIE. Man, who lives like that?

MILES. *(Trying to get rid of him.)* Yeah, right, thanks for your help, Reggie, I can get this from here.

REGGIE. You got ten more boxes out there.

MILES. I can handle it.

REGGIE. Where you gone lay them tiles down anyway, the kitchen? *(Miles hesitates, he knows where this is going.)*

MILES. I've got it all taken care of.

REGGIE. That will look nice, man. But you gotta take up all that linoleum, then you gotta patch up the holes and put something smooth down to glue the tiles to — you can't do all that by yourself.

MILES. Well, I have the time right now so I think I'll be alright.

REGGIE. We done did this in my mom's house in the eighties, man, I'm telling you — you gone need some help. Pulling that old stuff off piece by piece — ain't nothing for that but a pry bar. I don't *mind* an honest day's work. You hire some guy in the phonebook, he gone charge you two bills a day. I'll do it for half. *(Nina, wearing the baby in a sling, walks in carrying plastic bags loaded with groceries in both hands.)*

NINA. What's this — you bought tiles? How much did they cost? *(Miles glances at Reggie, wants to get rid of him. Miles reaches into his pocket and hands Reggie a five-dollar bill.)*

MILES. Here you go, man, thanks. *(Reggie looks at the money.)*

REGGIE. That's alright. We do it another way. *(Reggie heads out the door. Miles, embarrassed, puts the money back in his pocket.)*

MILES. Eric paid for the tiles, says it's his housewarming gift to us.

NINA. Miles, take the baby. You haven't held her since yesterday.

MILES. I don't want to wake her.

NINA. What about your interview this morning?

MILES. I went. *(Opens a box of tiles.)* Look, I got those tiles that you circled in the catalog —

NINA. Miles, how'd it go?

MILES. I don't want to take a job that I'm going to resent going to every day. You know what I really want to do.

NINA. Open a store with your brother? Miles, we make fun of your brother and his ridiculous schemes.

MILES. This isn't a scheme, it's a good idea.

NINA. I don't trust your brother, Miles. I'm sorry, but I don't. He doesn't have the experience —

MILES. He has tons of experience!

NINA. He's never opened a business here. He just goes to these Western-worshipping little Asian countries with his all-American good looks and he bamboozles them. He sells them shit.

MILES. How can you talk like that about my brother?

NINA. You don't need your brother. If you really want to start a business, then why don't you start something yourself?

MILES. Start a business — what business, with what? I don't have any ideas —

NINA. Look at what Reggie does, Reggie doesn't have anything but he's out on that street corner, paying attention to what's going on, looking for opportunities —

MILES. I'm not one of the guys on the corner, Nina. Are you telling me to stand on the corner with the rest of the unemployed black guys?

NINA. *No.*

MILES. This store is my idea. It's how I want to present myself to the community. A lot of these families living in these brownstones, they stayed committed to the community during the rough times. And now people like us are moving in and I want to be connected to their history. I don't want to be the intruder. I want to bring something. *(Mrs. Chae walks in. Miles and Nina brighten like school-children.)*

NINA and MILES. Good morning, Mrs. Chae. *(Mrs. Chae makes a beeline for the baby.)*

MRS. CHAE. She's asleep? You give me whole sling. This way you can work and I can keep Hannah while I do laundry. Yours too. *(Mrs. Chae picks up a few stray pieces of dirty clothing lying around.)*

NINA. Oh, you don't have to do that.

MRS. CHAE. I do this for my daughter. *(Mrs. Chae starts picking*

28

up stray laundry from around the living room.)

NINA. Huh … Do you … cook for her too?

MILES. Nina —

MRS. CHAE. Yes, of course. She and husband spend every weekend at my house. I cook a lots of food — *chap chae, bulgogi, kimchee chigae* — then Sunday, pack it up and they take home.

NINA. Man, I haven't had home-cooked Korean food in a long, long —

MRS. CHAE. You like the Korean food? Even the stinky kimchee?

NINA. I love kimchee. But I used to have to sneak it because my mom wouldn't let me eat it. She'd say, "You'll never have an American boyfriend."

MILES. Unless he eats kimchee too. *(Re: laundry.)* Let me get you something for that. *(He heads upstairs.)*

MRS. CHAE. Your mommy want you to have American boyfriend?

NINA. That's all we had where I grew up. Except for this one Filipino boy.

MRS. CHAE. I see. That's why she don't teach you the Korean language.

NINA. I don't think she knew I'd live in a place where I could speak Korean every day. Where every time my local Korean deli gets a new cashier, I have to explain no, I'm not Japanese, I'm Korean, I just can't talk to you.

MRS. CHAE. If you want, I teach you the Korean words I speak to Hannah.

NINA. Yes.

MRS. CHAE. That way you both learn together. And maybe someday I make kimchee for you. You work hard all day. You spend evening with Hannah instead of cook, clean and do laundry, eh? Hannah misses the mommy.

NINA. Do you think? Like, too much?

MRS. CHAE. She love the mommy and daddy. She talk about you all the time. *(Miles comes downstairs with a laundry bag.)*

MILES. Here you go, you can put things in here.

MRS. CHAE. Oh, thank you Miles. Such a good husband, hm? My husband, he never touch the laundry, never change the diaper, but Miles … he does so much. *(Mrs. Chae touches Miles' cheek, then goes upstairs. Eric opens the front door. Pushes in half a dozen large pieces of luggage.)*

MILES. You need a hand with that, man? *(He goes over to help.)*

NINA. What's going on, Eric?

ERIC. Miles was running out of clothes that fit me. Plus it was costing me twenty-one bucks a day to have this stuff in storage.

NINA. You took all of this to Malaysia?

ERIC. I was there for three months. I wanted to have my options.

MILES. I don't know if all that's gonna fit in the upstairs office.

ERIC. What about the basement? I don't need to put my hands on all this stuff every day. A bunch of these bags can go downstairs.

NINA. How long do you plan on staying here, if you don't mind my asking?

ERIC. Getting a store off the ground will take months, maybe a year. But, I don't have to stay here the whole time —

MILES. Where else are you going to stay?

ERIC. I can get a sublet —

NINA. It's just that we're still trying to get settled here —

MILES. I don't want you to do that, man. You're family.

NINA. Miles —

MILES. I asked him to stay here and help me launch the business. The least we can do is offer him a place to stay. We have the room —

NINA. No, we don't. That's supposed to be our office —

MILES. You have your office downstairs. The upstairs is my office and I say Eric is welcome to stay.

ERIC. I'm sorry, Nina, if I'd known you were against me staying here, I wouldn'ta brought all my [shit] —

NINA. This isn't personal, Eric, you just happen to have shown up at a time when we're … we're still trying to figure things out ourselves and … I just need to put my family first.

MILES. *(To Nina.)* Eric *is* family. *(To Eric.)* Come on, man, let's get these things upstairs.

Scene 7

Night. Eric sits at Nina's desk, Kit stands with her coat on, she's just come into the office.

KIT. Does Nina know you're down here?

ERIC. She's asleep. Why?

KIT. Well, she said she didn't want anyone else down here anymore.

ERIC. Oh —

KIT. Anyone except for me, her, Mrs. Chae and Hannah, of course … which only leaves you and Miles. *(Eric turns to the computer.)*

ERIC. I didn't know, I'll close my document right now.

KIT. *(Stopping him.)* So — what were you working on? Something to do with the store?

ERIC. I was drafting a proposal. Miles scoped out a great location. So, what do you think of our idea?

KIT. S'pretty good. Neighborhood's changing … yuppies love their pesto and their lattes, I know I do.

ERIC. You know, I don't know why Miles never had the idea to run his own business before.

KIT. It's a lot of extra work. And it doesn't always pay off. You know this.

ERIC. I just wonder if Miles leans on Nina too much. If she ends up holding him back. Because Miles — *(They hear a sound from the floor above.)* I should get out of here —

KIT. Go on.

ERIC. Miles can do anything, man.

KIT. He's smart and hardworking, he's creative —

ERIC. What? He's way more than that, man. Miles came into the world a four-pound, undernourished, heroin-addicted, premature little bird you could hold in the palm of your hand.

KIT. Miles was a heroin baby?

ERIC. His birth mother was some junkie, shot ten bags of dope to induce labor. Then after she gave birth, she snuck out of the hospital. My parents adopted him when he was still in the pediatric ICU.

KIT. I've known Nina and Miles for fifteen years, I've never heard that story.

ERIC. Ask Nina. When Miles was a kid, he had to go to physical therapy, occupational, speech … he rode the little special ed bus to school with the retards. And then in the fifth grade, pow! He just shot up and shot out. Next thing we knew he was doing karate, playing piano … writing code on the Commodore computer I got for Christmas.

KIT. Commodore. Your parents were cutting edge.

ERIC. All I did with it was play Pong so they ended up giving it to Miles. That's why I say he can do anything. And it's just … weird to come here and see him so …

KIT. Well, getting laid off right before you have a baby isn't exactly an ego booster.

31

ERIC. You're right.

KIT. I've watched Nina and Miles for a long time. They try to pass the power back and forth between them, but one person always ends up holding the ball. That's true with most relationships, it's true with two women. *(Beat.)*

ERIC. This is so embarrassing.

KIT. What?

ERIC. I'm such an idiot.

KIT. Why?

ERIC. Are you gay?

KIT. No!

ERIC. I thought ... because you said two women —

KIT. I'm talking about my friends Stephanie and Laura.

ERIC. OK, *good.*

KIT. Why would it have been embarrassing?

ERIC. Because ...

KIT. Yes?

ERIC. Because I hate to be wrong.

Scene 8

Office. The sound of scraping and prying from above — Miles and Reggie working on the floor. Kit and Nina work on the model — they are gluing on a cantilevered roof onto its beam. Kit applies the glue as Nina balances the top-heavy roof piece.

NINA. Your birthday already? What's today's date?

KIT. The third.

NINA. I completely lost track of time — OK, Thursday, your birthday. Is it — ... are you gonna be [forty?] —

KIT. Let's not touch on that.

NINA. OK. OK, what do you want to do? Do you want me to throw you a party?

KIT. *(Roof.)* Press down harder on this side.

NINA. Dinner with a bunch of our friends?

KIT. No.

NINA. Kit, you gotta ring it in. Your fortieth —

KIT. Do not speak the number.

NINA. You can't do nothing.

KIT. I don't want to do nothing. I want to go out to a nice, quiet dinner, just you and me. We can go to that new French place on DeKalb. It's close enough to here, you can be home in time to nurse Hannah.

NINA. You sure you don't want to go somewhere fabulous in Manhattan?

KIT. With you constantly checking your watch, worried that your breasts are going to explode?

NINA. I guess you're right. *(Kit finishes, leaves Nina holding the newly-glued-on piece.)*

KIT. So, Hannah being such a big baby and all, I was wondering — were you a big baby?

NINA. From the neck up. My body was skinny but my cheeks clocked in at about a pound each.

KIT. Miles must've been a big baby, then, huh?

NINA. Mm ... no. *(Kit, having hoped for a longer answer, fishes for more.)*

KIT. Have you ever seen pictures of him as a baby?

NINA. I have a picture of him when he was about one year old in my desk.

KIT. Can I see it?

NINA. Uh ... sure. It's in my top drawer. *(Kit opens Nina's top drawer, sifts around to find it. Looks at it.)*

KIT. Well. Looks like a perfectly healthy one-year-old to me. Perfectly healthy. *(She puts the photo back, goes to her desk, silently kicking herself for believing. Nina watches her, unsure what this is about.)*

NINA. Actually, a normal one-year-old should weigh about twenty pounds and Miles only weighed seventeen. *(Kit turns to Nina — enthused.)*

KIT. Tell me more.

NINA. His mom said he was a fussy eater — *(Kit's disappointment is visible.)*

KIT. ... Right.

NINA. He wouldn't drink milk or eat cheese which are good sources of fat. *(Nina looks at Kit, trying to read her reaction.)*

KIT. That makes sense. *(Beat.)*

NINA. Plus he was addicted to heroin for the first two months of his —

KIT. Yes!

NINA. You're in love with Eric! He told you about Miles. That's Miles' big secret.

KIT. It came up in conversation.

NINA. Pillow talk.

KIT. Eric and I haven't even gone out yet, let alone slept together. *(Half-beat.)*

NINA. Don't trust him, Kit.

KIT. What do you resent so much about Eric? Has he ever hurt you or Miles? *(Beat.)*

NINA. He's never there when it counts, you know, he didn't even come to our wedding. Then out of nowhere, he just swoops in and inserts himself into our lives. *(Mrs. Chae carries downstairs a tray with two bowls of soup.)*

MRS. CHAE. It's lunch time for the hardworking woman. *(She means "women.")*

NINA. *(Smelling, just saying it fills her.)* What is that? Seaweed soup? *(Mrs. Chae places a bowl on Nina's desk.)*

MRS. CHAE. *Mi yuk guk.* I write it down for you. Very good for the mommy after delivering the baby, because it has iron and protein. Good for you now because of the breastfeeding. You need the strength.

NINA. Thank you! I'll have it as soon as — *(Mrs. Chae places another bowl in front of Kit.)*

MRS. CHAE. Good for you too, because it also helps to make the baby. *(Kit gently pushes the soup bowl away from her.)*

KIT. Hmmmm … . Thanks … *(Mrs. Chae notices. So does Nina, she's embarrassed.)*

MRS. CHAE. Your husband don't want the children?

KIT. My husband … uh uh, he says he's not ready. *(Nina flashes her a look.)*

MRS. CHAE. You cannot wait for him. The man is never ready for the children, he is still his mommy's baby. But, having the child will make him a man.

NINA. You can still eat it, Kit, the soup won't impregnate you.

MRS. CHAE. *(To Nina.)* If you like, I teach you how to make it.

NINA. God, I would love that. *(Nina looks at the soup, she still can't move her hands. To Mrs. Chae:)* Would you mind moving that a little closer to me?

MRS. CHAE. Of course. *(Mrs. Chae does so. Nina leans her head down, without moving her hands, trying to get her mouth close enough to the bowl. She manages a sip.)*

NINA. Mm, smells fantastic. *(She blows on it. Mrs. Chae watches*

34

Nina struggle to drink the soup.) I'm dying to eat it but I can't move my hands until the glue — *(Mrs. Chae picks up the bowl, scoops up a spoonful of soup and blows on it before offering it to Nina.)*

MRS. CHAE. *(In Korean.)* Eat well.

NINA. Oh, gosh, um — *(Nina takes a sip of soup.)* Mm, that's delicious. *(Mrs. Chae continues to feed Nina.)*

MRS. CHAE. Soon it will be Hannah's *paek il.* We must have a big party.

NINA. *Paek il?* What's that?

MRS. CHAE. *Paek il* is for one hundredth day because back in old times, when a baby did not die by one hundred days, we have a big party. We say now she will live long life. *(Mrs. Chae feeds Nina another spoonful.)*

KIT. Where's Miles' camera when you need it?

NINA. Gosh, I really appreciate this but ... you don't have to feed me. *(We hear Miles' and Reggie's voices in disagreement.)*

MRS. CHAE. It's OK. Hannah is sleeping and I am in the way upstairs. Miles and his brother are working so hard.

NINA. Eric's helping? That's a shock.

MRS. CHAE. Yes. They are working together. *(Nina looks at Kit.)*

NINA. I thought he was going to the realtors — wait a second. Who do you mean by Miles' brother?

MRS. CHAE. The man, his brother. The one who's helping him.

NINA. Is he black?

MRS. CHAE. Yes.

NINA. That's not Miles' brother.

MRS. CHAE. Oh —

NINA. You met his brother. Eric. Eric's his brother. Reggie's ... just some *guy* who lives on our street. *(Kit notices Nina's tone of voice.)*

MRS. CHAE. Oh, I see ... *(A beat. Nina's uncomfortable.)* Miles is adopted?

NINA. Yes.

MRS. CHAE. *(A Korean sound.)* Oh ... *(Tsk tsk tsk.)* Such nice parents.

NINA. ... They're nice because they're white people who adopted a little black baby? *(Kit tastes the soup.)*

KIT. Mmmm, Mrs. Chae, this is good. What kind of seaweed is this?

MRS. CHAE. We call it mi yuk.

NINA. Because actually, I think Miles' parents were (.) they did things that were kind of ... like raising him in an all-white neighborhood, sending him to schools where he was the only black kid —

KIT. I thought you liked your in-laws —

NINA. Miles was teased a lot. The reason he'll be emotionally enslaved to Eric the rest of his life is because Eric would beat the shit out of kids who picked on him.

MRS. CHAE. But Miles grew up so nice. Clean and smart, handsome.

NINA. Did you just say [clean] —

KIT. Mrs. Chae, you mentioned your daughter has a child Hannah's age. Maybe he and Hannah can have a playdate! *(To Nina.)* It'd be good for Hannah to have another kid she can speak Korean to because ... you don't really have Korean friends ...

MRS. CHAE. *(Hesitates.)* I don't think —

NINA. What — you're afraid your daughter won't let him come because Hannah's black?

KIT. Nina —

MRS. CHAE. Hannah is not black. If you look at her, maybe you cannot tell. People cannot tell the daddy is black. She is just beautiful baby. *(Miles walks in through the outside door.)*

MILES. Nina, I've got to use your computer for a minute. *(He sits at her desk, launches a web browser.)*

NINA. Why can't you use your computer upstairs?

MILES. I told Reggie I was going to the hardware store to get something. I hid a little webcam so I can watch him. Mrs. Chae, do you mind staying down here for a few minutes?

KIT. Watch him do what?

MILES. Steal from me.

MRS. CHAE. *(A Korean expression of shock.)* Aigu.

NINA. Miles, you have no reason to think that Reggie stole your —

MILES. The man openly offered to sell me stolen goods, Nina. This is what he does. He insinuates himself into people's homes, and then he takes things he can sell. The gentrification of this neighborhood is the best thing to happen to him in years. *(Miles checks the web browser.)* See that — look, he's looking in one of our boxes. I put my portable DVD player in there on purpose. *(Nina looks.)*

NINA. This is wrong. I'm going upstairs to tell him —

KIT. Nina, don't let go of that — *(Nina starts for the stairs. Kit rushes to the model to grab the roof. Miles goes after Nina.)*

MILES. Nina, stay. I want to catch him.

NINA. You've set up a trap.

KIT. Look at it this way. If he doesn't take anything, you'll have won.

NINA. You approve of this?

36

KIT. No, I think it's sick but I admit it's pulled me in. *(Miles looks at the browser.)*
MILES. He's looking around … he's walking towards my ipod … he's picking up a pry bar — *(We hear the corresponding sound on the ceiling.)* And … he's pulling up the linoleum off the kitchen floor.
NINA. I am so embarrassed, Miles.
MILES. Well, someone took my camcorder.
NINA. You should go up there and apologize.
MILES. I'm not going to apologize. But I will let him keep working for us. And keep my eye on him. *(Miles goes out the front door.)*
MRS. CHAE. Can I … go upstairs now?
NINA. Yes. *(Mrs. Chae goes upstairs, Nina takes over the job of holding down the roof from Kit. Kit goes to her desk.)*
KIT. Do you want … me to feed you the soup?
NINA. No, I don't want it anymore. Do me a favor and throw it away.

Scene 9

The next day. Reggie holds one end of a tape measure while Miles pulls the rest across the length of the floor.

MILES. One hundred and thirty-five inches. Divided by two, that's sixty-seven and a half inches. *(He walks to that number on the measuring tape, then makes a mark on the floor.)* So this is the center of the room.
REGGIE. Why you doing this the hard way? All you have to do is start at this wall — *(Walks to border with living room.)* — get your tiles going across, then whenever you run into your fridge or your stove, you just cut the tile to fit. That's it.
MILES. No, if you do it that way then that's the only line that will look like full tiles. It's better to start in the center. That way I can distribute the error factor around the periphery of the room. *(After a beat.)* I'm going downstairs to ask Nina to take a look at —
REGGIE. Man, why do you have to — *(Miles turns to him.)* alright, alright, I get you, man. Now, I get you. I ain't never been married yet so I wasn't feeling you before, but now I am.
MILES. What?

REGGIE. 'Cuz I notice how you talk to your female, see what I'm saying. 'Cuz you always saying "I gotta ax Nina this," or "I can't 'til I ax Nina — " and I've been thinking, "What is this brother, hen-pecked or some shit?" But now I know that's how you do her to do you right. I'm'a try that shit myself.

MILES. Man, Nina's done this before.

REGGIE. I done this before! I keep telling you!

MILES. Nina's done this hundreds of times before. Not just once in her mother's house. Anyway, why are you still living in your mother's house?

REGGIE. She getting old, she need somebody.

MILES. Yeah, but, you never moved out, right? So, who's taking care of who?

REGGIE. I got four brothers and three sisters, seven nephews and eight nieces, we all there.

MILES. All living in that house?

REGGIE. We family, man. We got seventy-seven years history in that house. Ain't no yuppie gone come up in here and buy us out. *(Eric walks in.)*

ERIC. I tracked down the owner of the diner, he's this Hasidic guy who hangs out with his buddies in this bakery in Williamsburg. I made an appointment for Friday so you can meet him. *(Reggie starts arranging the tiles the way he wants them. Not gluing them, just placing them down to make a point.)*

MILES. Awesome.

REGGIE. "Awesome, dude."

ERIC. The landlord said another party approached him about the space last week. They want to open a tea lounge.

MILES. A tea lounge? Who around here is going to go to a tea lounge?

REGGIE. I would. I drink tea.

ERIC. To get an edge on these guys, I think we should put down a deposit. Are you ready to do that?

REGGIE. He gone ax his wife.

MILES. It's your money. If you want to be that aggressive —

ERIC. That's how you compete, little brother. You have to be fierce, you have to use that big brain of yours to think — how do I get the advantage? What idea can I come up with that no one else could.

MILES. I can do that.

ERIC. I'm gonna go to the bank tomorrow, convert my ringgits. *(Eric heads for the stairs just as Walter comes down. Once again, he goes straight out the door, without acknowledging anyone. Eric gives Miles a look — weird. As Eric goes upstairs, Nina comes up from the office. Reggie, having placed a few rows of tiles on the floor, seizes the opportunity.)*

REGGIE. *(To Nina.)* Mommy, look at this here. How this looks? You walk into the room, you see one solid line. That's the way to do it.

NINA. You're ... right, Reggie. That is ... a way to do it. But —

REGGIE. You hear that? She said I'm right. She said I'm right and she know more about this than you. But you ain't never said nothing like that.

MILES. Oh, Nina's your hero now?

NINA. Miles —

MILES. I've been telling you since the minute I met you that she's an architect. But you keep treating her like she doesn't know anything.

REGGIE. *(To Nina.)* Is that true? That ain't true. You the one who act like I don't know anything. I done did this before and you ain't. But you gotta be like one of them new niggas who always think — *(The baby starts crying upstairs. Nina can't decide whether to get the baby or stay with Miles.)*

MILES. No, man. No. I'm not any kind of nigger. You hear me?

REGGIE. Man, I ain't mean it like that. Over here when somebody say new nigga we mean somebody who turn they nose up at something 'cause it ain't new or good enough —

MILES. I don't care what you say it means, man. I don't want to hear it in my house. *(The baby's cries become jagged and intense. Nina can't take it anymore, goes upstairs to soothe the baby.)*

REGGIE. Man, you *all* new niggas to me, buying up these here brownstones for a million dollars when they done sat here for decades all boarded up — shit, city couldn't give these buildings away.

MILES. Don't try to give me that *back in the day bull* [shit] —

REGGIE. This house that you living in now had been abandoned so long it had a tree growing out of it — right through the roof. When we was little kids, we called it the tree house — *(Walks to window.)* We used to climb through that window and sit under the tree — *(Points to a spot on the floor.)* Right here — and smoke cigarettes, kiss, party, you name it. This was our house.

MILES. Man, don't try to make it sound like it was better back in the old days 'cause I know this house went on to be a shooting gallery and a crack house before the city took it over.

REGGIE. I ain't saying it was better. Shit, I got shot walking down

39

my street just going to buy some chicken wings at the Chinese restaurant. So I ain't saying nothing 'bout no back in the day. All I'm saying is — this is the way you do your tiles, son. You get them going across, ain't nothing else to worry about.

MILES. Reggie, man, if you want to help, I'll pay you. But we're gonna do it the way I want it. OK? You had your good times but it's my house now. *(Beat.)*

REGGIE. *(Checks watch.)* I gotta go check on my girl, wake her ass up otherwise she ain't gone get to work — *(He goes out the door. Nina comes downstairs carrying Hannah.)*

NINA. Miles, is everything OK?

MILES. Where's Mrs. Chae? Why isn't she here taking care of the baby?

NINA. I told her to come in a little later this morning. I think we have a problem.

MILES. What're you talking about? She seems to be working out great. *(Eric hurries downstairs carrying a pair of boxer shorts.)*

ERIC. This is fucked up, man. This is out of line, this is fucked up.

MILES. What's going on, man?

ERIC. My ringgits are gone.

MILES and NINA. What? *(He holds out his boxer shorts.)*

ERIC. I hid the money in here — I folded these up and put them underneath the mattress in the sofa bed. I figured we were all family here.

MILES. Man, what is going on around here?

ERIC. You got a lot of new people coming in and out of this house. The tenant passes by all our bedrooms to get to his floor. He's got a lock on the door to his apartment, but all our rooms are wide open. Maybe he took your camcorder. What do you know about that guy?

MILES. Not much.

ERIC. If you ask me — you guys need to close ranks. Clean house. How much is he paying in rent?

NINA. Twelve hundred a month.

ERIC. I could pay that. Or close to that. I've got some money in the bank, plus I've built in salaries for me and you in the business proposal. *(Nina looks at Miles — you're not going for this, are you?)*

MILES. We can't just kick him out, we gave him a two-year lease.

ERIC. I should be part of this community too. It'll be good for the profile of the business.

MILES. We'll see what we can do to make that happen, man.

NINA. We will?

ERIC. Let me go upstairs and have another look. *(He goes upstairs.)*

NINA. *(To Miles.)* We need twelve hundred for the upstairs apartment. I cannot meet our mortgage payments without — I can't take it on, Miles. I can't have one more thing on my back.

MILES. It's not going to be on your back. Eric said he's going to pay rent.

NINA. No, he's not. Eric came here with the intention of getting us to give him a free place to live.

MILES. He came here to meet the baby.

NINA. We haven't seen or heard from him in months —

MILES. He just got off a plane.

NINA. Then on the day we move in, he shows up at our doorstep with no place to live. He comes up with this business idea, says he's got the money to get it started, gets you all riled up about it, then all of a sudden — the money's gone. He never had the money, Miles.

MILES. You never saw it, but I saw it.

NINA. He probably bought it at a party store with a pack of tropical drink umbrellas. What bothers me the most, Miles, is that we've always laughed at your brother ... together, we've indulged him, we'd listen to his stories and wink wink at each other knowing that it was all a big show ... but now I look over at you, and you're rapt. You're like a kid listening to his con man uncle and hanging on every word. *(Hannah starts to cry.)*

MILES. You think that I'm that stupid?

NINA. I think you're ... vulnerable, I think you're groping for something to hold onto, someone ... and you've latched onto your brother instead of me and Hannah. We're your family now. *(Nina tries to hand Miles the baby. He doesn't take her.)*

MILES. No, she only cries harder.

NINA. Only when she senses your fear. Just focus on how much you love her, and she'll calm down.

MILES. You know she's going to reject me.

NINA. No, she won't.

MILES. She only wants you. I don't have anything she needs.

NINA. Miles, take her —

MILES. No, you want me to fail. You want me to. *(He storms off. Nina turns to Hannah.)*

NINA. It's OK, sweetie, Daddy loves you. Of course Daddy loves you.

Scene 10

Office. Kit is working, Nina is nursing Hannah.

KIT. Nina, you can't take time away from work to look for a new nanny. I won't let you.

NINA. It won't take that long, I'm not going to hold out for a Korean woman. I'll take anyone who isn't going to poison my baby with racist thoughts.

KIT. You're blowing this whole thing out of proportion.

NINA. I'm not. I know that as sure as someday Hannah's going to fall off her bike and scrape her knee, that someone is going to call her a chink, and a nigger —

KIT. Cover her ears!

NINA. I can't stop it. I can't protect her from it — I can't stop it from happening to me as a grown woman. Last month, I was standing in the front lawn of my childhood home, where I used to play cowboys and Indians, and ride my banana seat Schwinn, and some teenager shouted from a car, "Go back to Vietnam — "

KIT. It's horrible, it's embarrassing, but I still think that's completely different from what Mrs. Chae —

NINA. My whole bright idea about hiring a Korean nanny was to give Hannah a reason to be proud to be Korean. I thought if she could, I don't know, speak the language, have some sense of belonging — it would help those names bounce off of her. We had the same reasons for wanting to raise Hannah in a mostly black neighborhood.

KIT. Look, you guys are making great choices for her —

NINA. No, we're not, we're failing in every way. The Korean nanny's denying her blackness, the black neighbors are throwing rocks through our window ... Miles won't hold our baby and ... I see how hard you're working and I'm trying my best — I know I'm not pulling my weight — but I swear I am giving this *everything* I have left. And all I ask from Miles, all I want him to do ... *(A beat for Nina.)* ... is to be in it with me. *(Nina covers her mouth to hide that she's crying — something she saw her mother do.)*

KIT. Hey — *(Kit walks over, kneels in front of Nina.)*

NINA. But instead, he wants to know when we're going to start

42

having sex again. And I can't — I swear, Kit, I don't have anything left to give. *(Nina hides her face by nuzzling Hannah.)*

KIT. When we're in Barcelona, I'm gonna take you to this fantastic little tapas place I read about. We'll eat little plates of fried octopus eyes and beef snout on toast while we watch them build our building. We're going to make the deadline, I'll make sure of it. *(Nina nods but aims all her need at Hannah, kissing her, holding her close. Kit goes to touch Nina supportively, but Nina has closed the circle — there's only room for her and her baby. Kit stands up, walks back to her drawing table. She draws for a minute.)*

NINA. Eric tell you about the missing money?

KIT. I heard about it.

NINA. What do you think? Do you think someone really stole it?

KIT. I think it's a ghost. I think that first night when your window got smashed, the ghost of all the neglected communities past — who couldn't get the city to fix their sidewalks, or keep their electricity going on hot days, let alone provide them with a local source of organic half-and-half — wafted in here and is trying to spook you into leaving. *(Kit puts something down on the table, Nina picks it up — a matchbook from a restaurant.)*

NINA. What's this?

KIT. It has the restaurant's name and address on DeKalb. The food was good, you and Miles should go there some time.

NINA. What? Ohmigod. Oh please God, please please please let it not be —

KIT. It's new, so it's not that crowded yet. They let me sit for a while.

NINA. You waited for me? Why didn't you call?

KIT. I have some dignity, you know.

NINA. Why didn't you remind me during the day!

KIT. Just, let it pass, Nina.

NINA. No, it's totally my fault. I can't believe I forgot to show up for your fortieth birth [day] —

KIT. Just stop talking about it, OK? I don't care that you didn't show up, I don't care. I ate dinner, went to a bar, fucked a guy in the bathroom — it was perfect. The best birthday ever. All I want from you, Nina, is for you to do your work. Fucking do your work. I can't finish this model by myself, not with less than six weeks left. I waited for you, Nina, I could've started two months ago without you, but you told me to wait.

NINA. I shouldn't have done that. It's just — I never ... it's like this feral — this animal drive to take care of my daughter. I can't even apologize for it, it fucking feels right.

KIT. So you shouldn't be trying to work.

NINA. I want to work. I don't want to be a stay-at-home mom. I know it doesn't add up, OK? But I still love my work.

KIT. Look, Nina, you're a good mom — my mom, she took Dexatrim when she was pregnant with me because she didn't want to get fat. And I — I don't think women should have children if they're not going to be like you. But this work is all I have and I fucking want to win this competition.

NINA. I do too.

KIT. Don't say that.

NINA. I know it doesn't make sense —

KIT. Nina, I'm forty years old, I already don't have what I thought I would have by now but I know I can make beautiful buildings. It's not fucking fair for you to hold me back. Between Mrs. Tillman's unreasonable demands and your constant distractions, we're way behind already.

NINA. I'll take care of Mrs. Tillman.

KIT. No, you won't.

NINA. When she calls today, tell her I'll meet her at the house.

KIT. That's nice of you to finally offer, but Mrs. Tillman isn't going to call today because I told her we quit.

NINA. What — ?

KIT. This morning, she insisted I go all the way to the Upper East Side just to show me some dust from the living room had "pene-trated" her bedroom. And I just — I fucking had it.

NINA. You quit — you — ... you quit before she finished paying us?

KIT. Now we can focus on the model.

NINA. Kit — how could you do that to me?

KIT. We need to concentrate on the model.

NINA. Mrs. Tillman is my livelihood. That money is what my family lives on.

KIT. We split the money but I do all the work.

NINA. I designed the plans with you. I did my share until the baby was born. (*Nina thinks a beat, looks at the baby, then picks up her bag. Calling upstairs:*) Mrs. Chae? (*To Kit.*) I'm going to apolo-gize to Mrs. Tillman.

KIT. Go ahead.

NINA. (*Yells.*) Mrs. Chae! (*To Kit.*) I'm getting this job back, Kit.

KIT. Fine, *you* can run up there every time a nail gets hammered in crooked.

NINA. Mrs. *Chae! (Mrs. Chae rushes downstairs.)*

MRS. CHAE. Sorry, Nina, I could not hear you.

NINA. I need you to take Hannah right now.

MRS. CHAE. Yes, yes, I will take. *(Mrs. Chae reaches for the baby, says in Korean, "It's OK, baby, Mommy is very busy so Grandma will take care of you.")*

NINA. What did you just say?

MRS. CHAE. Mh?

NINA. What did you say to her?

MRS. CHAE. I say you are very busy, so I will take her upstairs —

NINA. Did you call yourself *"halmoni"*?

MRS. CHAE. ... Yes?

NINA. Grandma?

MRS. CHAE. In Korean language, a child will call any woman my age —

NINA. When I come back, we need to talk. *(Nina flies out the door.)*

KIT. I'm sorry —

MRS. CHAE. *(Consoling herself, but aiming it at Hannah.)* It's OK, it's OK, I know everything will be OK. *(Mrs. Chae heads upstairs as Eric walks in through the front door. He walks up to Kit, stands close to her.)*

ERIC. Hey.

KIT. Hi.

ERIC. Now I know why you take a car service, it's a bitch to get here from your house by train. Do you feel hungover?

KIT. Eric, I don't have the money.

ERIC. You didn't get to stop by the bank on your way in?

KIT. No.

ERIC. Well, you still have a couple hours —

KIT. I'm not going to loan you any money. I'm sure both of us said things last night that we don't intend to follow through on. We were drunk, we were having a good time —

ERIC. You called me up, lured me to that restaurant with your sob story —

KIT. I invited you to join me, you ordered the most expensive thing on the menu, I picked up the tab ... everything that happened after that was fun, but it wasn't worth five thousand dollars. You're just going to have to tell your brother you never had the money.

ERIC. I had the money. I had it until last night.

KIT. Well, I'm sure you'll find a way around it, Eric, you're fast on your feet.

Scene 11

Living room. Miles comes downstairs in a suit and jacket —
he's missing a tie. He starts looking through some boxes, pulling
out kitchen utensils from one box, winter clothes from another
... Eric comes downstairs wearing a dress shirt and tie.

ERIC. You look sharp, man.

MILES. I'm looking for my ties —

ERIC. You don't need a tie, you look crisp without one. *(Miles lifts*
a box off the top of a stack and looks in the box underneath it.)

MILES. I want to make a strong appearance, those tea lounge people probably wear thrift store T-shirts and flip-flops.

ERIC. Don't bring up the tea lounge unless he brings it up first.
As far as I know, they haven't put down any money so we'll be on
even ground. *(Miles pulls his camcorder out of a box.)*

MILES. My camcorder ... that's what I did with it. I put it in here
after Reggie came in with his chandelier and was roaming all over
the place.

ERIC. Well, alright. That's great. *(A beat.)*

MILES. So, if my camcorder was never stolen ...

ERIC. What?

MILES. What happened to your ringgits?

ERIC. I don't know, man.

MILES. Eric ... tell me straight up. Were those ringgits real?

ERIC. Of course they were real.

MILES. Where are they, man, I don't believe Walter took them.

ERIC. Oh, I think he has them.

MILES. Eric —

ERIC. What you want to do is watch his checking account. You
have all his information from his credit report, right? Watch his
account for the next couple weeks and you just might see a deposit
for five grand show up. *(Beat.)*

MILES. Then, what, he's going to tell me he's moving out?

ERIC. Could be.

MILES. Is that what you did with the money, Eric? You wanted
me and Nina to think Walter stole it, but really you paid him so he

would move out? *(Beat.)*

ERIC. I offered it to him, yeah.

MILES. Man — that money was supposed to be for our business.

ERIC. You want me to commit to this business but what're you doing for me? You own this whole brownstone, but you'd rather price-gouge a stranger than give your brother a home.

MILES. We need to make ends meet.

ERIC. You always make ends meet, Miles. Why're you acting like you don't know that everything's gonna turn out your way — it always does.

MILES. You think things just snap into place — ?

ERIC. Nina's gonna win her competition, the store's going to be an instant success, Hannah's gonna be the poster baby for the new Benetton campaign ... you're going to have it all, like you always do — why do you have to deny me a piece of it?

MILES. Man, I've earned what I have. This is what I've always worked for. But you've been flitting around the world, cobbling together this little job with that one, never building anything, never digging roots, and now you're looking at me and saying "I want some of that"?

ERIC. You don't think I want this? A house, a steady career and a family? What do you think I am, a circus performer? A pirate? Of course I want those things but I've never been able to work for them because I'm not allowed to have what Miles has. Miles is the super baby, the poor little black boy left on our doorstep who goes on to save the town and my job in life is to make sure I never over-shadow him.

MILES. Mom and Dad gave you every chance they gave me. They cut everything straight down the line.

ERIC. You want to think things were that way, but they weren't. You were always the golden boy, the miracle ... I could never live up to it, Miles.

MILES. Did you try? All *you* had to do was try.

ERIC. What, because I'm white? Because I know who my biological parents are, because I can walk down the street of our hometown without some old lady calling the cops — you think that every door in the world is open to me? They're not, Miles. The doors are for you.

MILES. Do you know what it is like for me to look at my baby, and see her brown skin, and curly hair, and long eyelashes and know she got them from me — but I don't know who I come from? What am I giving her? What have I passed on? I don't know.

Maybe there's some disease that skips a generation, and I've given it to her. Or maybe my great-great-grandfather was a Civil War hero, but I'll never be able to tell Hannah about it. All I can do is take her to Mom and Dad's house in Indiana, where Mom can explain every little tchochke and how it was handed down to her … and dad can break out the family albums going back seven generations — but when she looks at those people in the photographs, she won't see herself, she won't see me.

ERIC. You think I see myself in those old pictures? All I see are a bunch of old people in stiff suits who had sixteen children and were half-dead from lung cancer by the time they were our age.

MILES. That's how you make it hard for yourself, Eric. Trying to invent yourself from scratch.

ERIC. You did. Why don't you think you're history enough for Hannah? *(Nina walks upstairs, notices the camcorder.)*

NINA. You found the camcorder.

MILES. … Yeah.

NINA. Where was it?

MILES. … Where I put it.

ERIC. I'm gonna go to this meeting, man.

NINA. Miles, I want to fire Mrs. Chae this afternoon.

ERIC. Catch up with me if you can … *(Eric leaves.)*

Scene 12

Living room. Mrs. Chae crosses the living room to get to the door, Miles sees her.

MILES. Mrs. Chae, are you leaving?

MRS. CHAE. Yes.

MILES. You left your lunch —

MRS. CHAE. Not my lunch. It's jap chae for you and Nina. You have it for dinner. *(She heads for the door.)*

MILES. You'll still be with us for two more weeks, right?

MRS. CHAE. I am old woman with nothing to do. Husband is dead, no job, what I'm going to do?

MILES. I — I don't know what to say, you've been wonderful to

48

Hannah … but —

MRS. CHAE. I try so hard, I want to make you and Nina happy. What have I done so wrong? *(Nina walks upstairs from the office, having overheard the last part. Mrs. Chae takes a step towards her.)* Nina — *(Without thinking, Mrs. Chae speaks to Nina in Korean:)* Nina, you're such a good girl, hm? Give me another chance. I'll do everything right.

NINA. I don't. Understand you.

MRS. CHAE. You are good girl, such a good mommy, hm? Best mommy. My daughter, she hire the British nanny to take care of my grandson. She tell me she don't want Mommy to take care of grandson. She don't want grandson to speak the bad English like Mommy. Kyung Soon say when she was little girl, she speak the English like Mommy, go to school and say "preejing," it's "pree-jing" outside. And children laugh laugh.

NINA. … Pleasing?

MRS. CHAE. So cold, it's preejing and Kyung Soon come home and say, "Mommy, you are dummy. You are such dummy!"

MILES. … Kids …

MRS. CHAE. So, she hire another nanny, not me. British nanny take care of my grandson.

NINA. You said your daughter has her son in daycare at her firm?

MRS. CHAE. Now I am telling you. British nanny comes at seven o'clock in morning, stay until eight o'clock at night. Then, Tibetan nanny comes on weekend, so Kyung Soon and husband can play golf.

MILES. She has two nannies?

MRS. CHAE. Yes.

MILES. That's a lot of nannies.

NINA. So … you've been lying about all of that?

MRS. CHAE. I tell you the truth now. Before, I want[ed] you to hire me, I see nice family, two good parents — happy baby … I want[ed] to be in this house, I want[ed] to be in this [family] … *(Miles turns to Nina.)*

MILES. Nina, maybe firing her isn't the right thing to do.

NINA. *(To Mrs. Chae.)* I know people like you. Some of my mom's friends, they came to this country in the sixties, white people taunted them, told them their food stank, their faces were flat, called them gook, chink, chingaling —

MILES. *(To Nina.)* Whoa —

NINA. Made them feel like shit for what, for walking down the street, for sending their kids to school, for starting a business. For

49

that they got beaten up, their stores got vandalized, right?

MRS. CHAE. ... Yes. My husband and I had gift store in Yonkers. Somebody paint all over the windows.

NINA. So what did you do?

MRS. CHAE. We cleaned the windows. My husband and I scrubbed the paint off with our hands —

NINA. You went looking for someone you could feel superior to. And you picked black people.

MILES. Nina, I think you need — you need to take a step back.

NINA. It makes me mad, it makes me ashamed of being Korean, fucking racists.

MILES. Mrs. Chae is new to this country, she's from another generation ... I don't like what she said to Hannah but I don't think she's a racist —

NINA. Bullshit. My mom was all those things and she never said anything like that. Even in that shitty little town we lived in. Mrs. Chae is from Queens, she has no excuse.

MILES. Well, she'll learn —

NINA. Who taught my mom — nobody. It was in her heart. *(Half beat.)*

MILES. Oh, I get it. I get it now, Nina. It's like you hired Mrs. Chae to be your mom. And you're firing her because she's not.

NINA. Geezus, Miles, is it too much to ask you to take my side?

MILES. Side — !? What do you want this to be, Nina?

NINA. I want you to ... I want you to defend me. *(Miles looks at Mrs. Chae, who has kept her head down, turns back to Nina.)*

MILES. Nobody's attacking *you!*

NINA. That's not the point.

MILES. *(To Mrs. Chae.)* Excuse her, Mrs. Chae, Nina's under a tremendous amount of press[ure] —

MRS. CHAE. She is working very hard. *(Moves towards Nina, who turns to Miles.)*

NINA. Don't fucking apologize for me.

MILES. You just said you wanted me —

NINA. Not to apologize, I want you to — Christ, if you think I'm being unreasonable —

MILES. Yes!

NINA. Then, fucking ... hold me or something.

MILES. You're not making me want to hold you.

NINA. I have to do something — ?

MILES. Well, you're not making me feel like it —

NINA. So, making all the money for the family doesn't qualify me for a hug?

MILES. Why d'you — *(Looks at Mrs. Chae.)* Why d'you have to say that?

NINA. Because I'm tired of having to tiptoe around your ego. My work is totally stressful, I'm not giving the baby the time I want — but at the end of the day, I don't get to vent to you. If I say anything about the pressure that is fucking crushing me — you think I'm trying to make you feel bad.

MILES. So, what, you're discounting the fact that most of the down payment for this house came from cashing in my stock options?

NINA. I'm not counting money, I could give a shit about the money —

MILES. This is obviously about money, you resent me for not being able to provide for my daughter. Look at this house — it's crumbling down around us. We can't afford to fix it, we can't afford to live in it. This is no way to raise a baby. We never should have ... we were not ready to have a baby. *(Kit walks upstairs.)*

KIT. *(To Nina.)* Is everything OK?

NINA. You're blaming me because we have a healthy, beautiful baby?

MILES. No, I'm blaming you because we have a baby that I don't deserve.

NINA. She needs you to love her, Miles.

MILES. It's not enough. *(The doorbell rings. Reggie appears on the other side of the broken window.)*

REGGIE. Hey yo, son, I got the guys with the glass, they gonna install it.

NINA. *(Looks at Miles.)* Now? They were supposed to have come at two, here they are at six-thirty.

MRS. CHAE. That's Korean time.

MILES. You deal with this, Nina, I'm — *(He heads upstairs.)*

NINA. *(Calling after him.)* You're what? *(Miles continues upstairs. Nina looks at Mrs. Chae.)* Fuck him, man, fuck all of you. I had this perfect, precious baby and all anyone wants to do is blame me for how she's changed our lives. Of course she's changed our lives. What was so fucking good about them before? *(Reggie knocks on the front door then opens it.)*

REGGIE. *(To Nina.)* Yo, mommy, they gone have to take the rest of that old glass out first. So I'm'a have to put some drop cloth down there so you don't get no glass shards on the floor.

NINA. OK, Reggie. *(A beat.)*

REGGIE. I'm'a go to the hardware store, so, you gone have to hit me so I can get the drop cloth.

NINA. *(Handing him a twenty.)* Here.

REGGIE. I'm'a need sixty.

NINA. Sixty dollars for drop cloth?

REGGIE. OK, forty.

NINA. I don't have forty dollars, Reggie.

KIT. I have forty dollars. *(Reaches into wallet.)* Oh, no, I don't.

NINA. *(To Mrs. Chae.)* Do you have any money?

MRS. CHAE. Sorry.

NINA. Just — fuck it, Reggie.

REGGIE. Alright, thirty dollars, I'll get the cheap stuff.

NINA. Forget it — forget the whole thing. Tell the guys they have to come back another — *(Smash. The sound of the workmen smashing the glass [to make way for the new window].)* Goddamnit — !

REGGIE. What the fuck! Stupid motherfucker! *(He heads for the door. Another smash. Nina releases a sound — something between a growl and a war cry. She picks up a prybar and walks to the window and starts smashing it as Kit and Mrs. Chae try to stop her. Reggie, on the other side, backs up. Nina gets a couple whacks in until she hears the sound of Hannah crying. Nina takes a breath, her demeanor changes. Mrs. Chae also responds to the sound. They both head for the stairs —)*

NINA. *(To Mrs. Chae.)* I'll get her. *(She just gets to the stairs when Miles appears at the top of the stairs holding the baby.)*

MILES. I got her. *(He walks downstairs towards Nina. Knows the words.)* "Hush little baby, don't say a word. Papa's gonna buy you a mockingbird. If that mockingbird won't sing, Papa's gonna buy you a diamond ring." *(He meets up with Nina.)* You want me to teach you the rest of the words?

NINA. Yes.

MILES. *(Sings.)* "If that diamond ring turns brass." *(Nina repeats after him as they walk towards the window.)*

NINA. *(Sings.)* "Turns brass."

MILES. *(Sings.)* "Papa's gonna buy you a looking-glass."

NINA. *(Sings.)* " — looking-glass."

MILES. *(Sings.)* "If that looking-glass gets broke — " *(They stop at the window. They look out into the street for a while. We start to hear the sounds of the neighborhood. Indeterminate voices in conversation. A basketball being bounced, music from a car stereo.)*

NINA. *(Looks at baby.)* She's looking at you.

MILES. *(Looks too.)* She likes my voice.

NINA. Yes.

MILES. And she likes the way I'm holding her. See? She stopped crying when I pressed her against my chest.

NINA. She can feel your heartbeat. *(Miles checks. Hannah's feet are against his chest.)*

MILES. With her feet? *(He turns the baby around.)* Now she can hear.

NINA. *(Looks out.)* You know what I think this hole in our window's for?

MILES. No, what?

NINA. To let out all the dust and ghosts that have been trapped in here.

MILES. There's too many old stories floating around.

NINA. It's our house now.

End of Play

PROPERTY LIST

Boxes of stuff
Pizza
Plates
Cell phone
Beers
Rock
Plywood, tools
Camera
Blue currency
Baby Björn
Chandelier
Paper
Computer
Architectural model, model pieces, glue
Keys
Bag of food
Purses
Boxes of tiles
Plastic bags with groceries
Wallet, money
Laundry, laundry bag
Large suitcases
Photo
Tray with two bowls of soup, spoons
Tape measure
Boxer shorts
Matchbook
Camcorder
Crowbar

SOUND EFFECTS

Baby crying
Gurgling
Bang
Cell phone
Glass smashing
Doorbell
Office phone
Car horn
Scraping and prying
Street noises